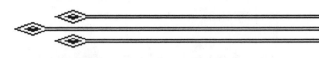

FURNITURE OF THE ARTS & CRAFTS PERIOD

"STICKLEY"

LIMBERT, MISSION OAK, ROYCROFT, FRANK LLOYD WRIGHT, AND OTHERS

WITH PRICES

EDITED BY:
L-W BOOK SALES

© COPYRIGHT 1992

L-W BOOK SALES
P.O. BOX 69
GAS CITY, IN 46933

ISBN# 0-89538-011-0

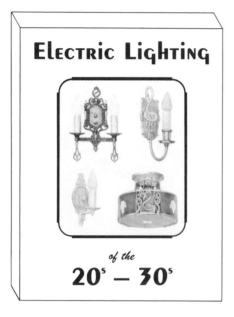
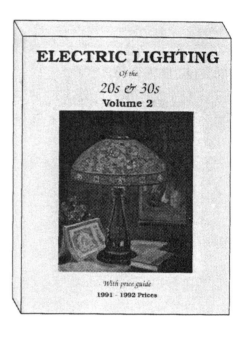

Cover Design: David Devon Dilley
Interior Design: Jamison Miller
Interior Layout: Jamison Miller, Denny Smith, & David Dilley

Published by:
L-W Book Sales
P.O. Box 69
Gas City, IN 46933

ISBN# 0-89538-011-0

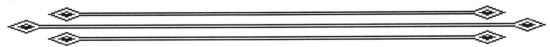

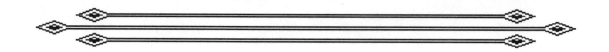

Dedication

This book was made possible by Treadway Galleries of Cincinnati, Ohio. Don Treadway was farsighted enough to see a definitive need for a photo book on Arts & Crafts Furniture with Prices.

Every piece pictured in this book was sold by Treadway Galleries. Again we wish to thank Don Treadway for without him this book would not be possible.

Remember if you have any of the items to sell either outright or at auction, contact Treadway's Gallery at (513) 321-6742, in Chicago call John Toomey at (708) 383-5234

Table of Contents

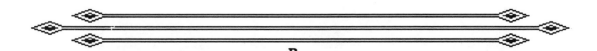

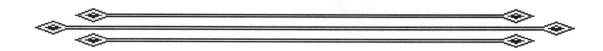

Introduction

   Welcome to the realm of early Nineteenth-Century quality craftsmanship. This manual will provide a refreshing insight into these days gone by, when the durable quality and simple beauty combined with practicality was a standard not ignored by the craftsmen of this era. This is proven to be absolutely true, as these pieces sculpted from wood & ingenuity and basked in fine stain & artistic care are still being used and sought after to this day.

   Perhaps it is the dream of our forefathers enjoying these furnishings years ago while they relaxed at their home that captures our attention of these desirable relics. Maybe it is a reaction to our disgust at contemporary pieces that lack the warmth, care, and meticulous workmanship that breathed life into the monuments of this period. Whatever the reasons, this manual is devoted to America's proudest features from it's Arts & Crafts movement. Stickley, Limbert & Roycroft are but a small handful of the producers of the types of furniture that are represented in this book. While there is some literature available on this subject that is purely informative in nature, this book will offer an up to date pricing guidelines and other neccessary data that should be helpful to modern collectors.

   As proud as these furniture makers were to embellish all of their work with their individual markings, we are proud to offer the contents of this book to any collector or aficionado who is interested in the great historical and artistic significance of this period.

The Editors

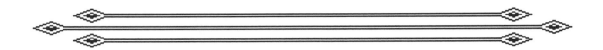

The following is the introduction to
L. & J.G. Stickley catalog of the early teen's.

The numerous pieces that furnish your house - the Chairs, the Tables, the oaken Settles, Sideboards and all the others- are undoubtedly THINGS ! Yes, but if you choose each piece with due regard to your individual needs and preferences, if you carefully create an environment of furniture; each piece of it then becomes, not a THING, but an undeniable part of yourself !

Individuality

L. & J.G. Stickley, makers of the simple and entirely American type of furniture that bears their impress, are working for individuals. Each year sees many new designs taking shapes of wood and leather in their shops, built, every one of them, to take an intimate place in some household or to serve someone in a public building; skillfully contrived, that is, to fit an individual need.

Harmony

You demand in your house, in your office or in your public building, a certain well-defined harmony. Wall treatment, floors, furniture, must all harmonize in color and pattern, must bear a subtle relationship to each other. In response to this demand of yours for harmony, the furniture illustrated in this book is planned and fashioned to fit into your scheme, whatever that may be.

Woods

White oak, the wood chiefly used, is selected not only for strength and durability, but on account of a capacity for taking on various shades and tones of color.

Design

This oak, cut in the forests of Kentucky, is built into furniture strong and durable, though not over heavy, suitable for your office, bank, or for the more formal rooms of your house; or slighter shapes are wrought from the oak, showing in their details graceful curves and variations of surface, perhaps bits of inlay in the same wood; or again the oak is turned into a little masterpiece of downright invention.

Finishes

A design fitted for some particular need of yours decided upon (and there are whole groups of furniture with the same motive running through them, suitable for use together in a room) the question of harmonizing color and finish is developed in the L. & J.G. Stickley Shops. And in this field of endeavor Leopold Stickley, "L" of the firm, one of the well known family of master workers in wood , has through several years of study and experiment arrived at expert knowledge of possible colors and undertones, treating the oak through fuming and staining, producing beauty of color as rich and glowing as that found upon certain old canvases.

Texture

Fumed by ammonia in air-tight compartments, and stained in tones that show beautiful undertints, the furniture is next given, through sanding and waxing, a smooth bloom-like texture, so that the arm or back of your chair is delightful to the touch.

Leathers

In treating the leathers used as covering for chair cushions or table tops, colors harmonizing or contrasting with those of the furniture are obtained, giving the needful accents to your color scheme. Old time methods of tanning are used, and no injurious acids impair the strength of the leather. Goat skins, not long since on their former owners, roaming the meadows of Palestine, thus contribute to the beauty and comfort of your rooms, since the skins used in the Work of L. & J.G. Stickley come from those sections of the Holy Land where the finest goats in the world are grown. Native hides are used for large table tops, and fabrics plain and figured are occasionally employed for cushion coverings.

Metal Work

Where hinges and pulls are needed, as upon chests of drawers and bookcases, these metal fixtures are of copper handwrought in simple designs. The copper is hammered to obtain texture and is dulled and modulated in color by various processes until the soft tones of old metal are secured.

Details of Construction

How your furniture is built is a matter of vital importance to you. Furniture of simple and good construction does not go out of style in a few years, but lasts your lifetime. The Work of L. & J.G. Stickley, built in a scientific manner, does not attempt to follow the traditions of bygone day. All the resources of modern invention are used as helps in constructing this thoroughly modern product, more suitable, as many notable authorities believe, to the house of to-day - your house, that is - than is the furniture of past centuries or its necessarily machine made reproductions.

If you examine the table legs and those of the large chairs built at the L. & J.G. Stickley Shops, you will find that each side of the post is quarter sawed. If you should investigate further and cut a cross section through the post, you will find that it is not veneered but built of four pieces of solid oak, with a tiny core, all so tightly welded together that no cracking is possible, and the post is practically indestructible, while the fine silver flake of quartering is seen from any point of view. Table tops, necessarily constructed, in these days of narrow boards, of several pieces of lumber, are fastened together by "splines" or tiny wedges as you see in the drawing or in your table top, so that no splitting is possible, the splines giving an agreeable bit of structural ornament.

Details of Construction

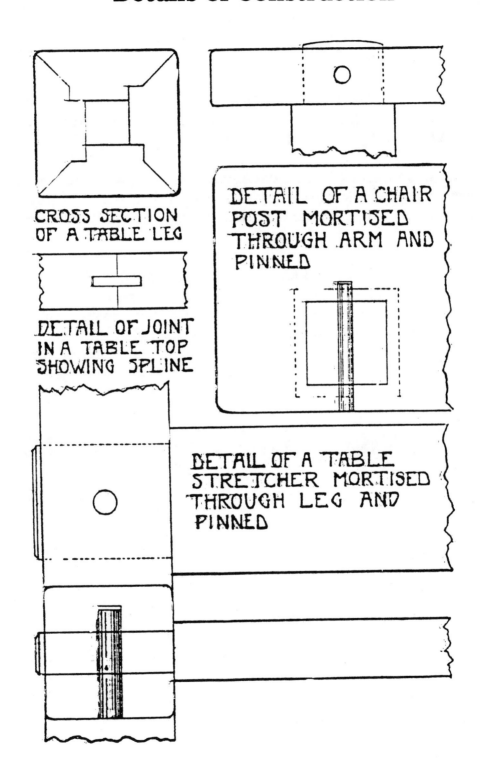

CROSS SECTION
OF A TABLE LEG

DETAIL OF JOINT
IN A TABLE TOP
SHOWING SPLINE

DETAIL OF A CHAIR
POST MORTISED
THROUGH ARM AND
PINNED

DETAIL OF A TABLE
STRETCHER MORTISED
THROUGH LEG AND
PINNED

Comfort

In these details and in many others care is given to your comfort, as well as to the durability of each piece of furniture. Chairs are studied from the point of view of many different sitters, and are of many sizes and proportions. In planning the height of tables, and especially of desks, an average is not struck. Heights suitable to various individuals are carefully planned.

The Makers Have no Other Occupation

The Work of L. & J.G. Stickley is a product that claims and fills the entire time of its producers, who indulge in no other occupation, rightly thinking that each process, from the proper seasoning of the timber to the exact color to be attained in the finished piece, must be watched to guard against the slightest measure of failure and to secure the greatest possible efficiency of method. Furniture building, it is believed, is in itself an important work, demanding the entire time of the modern craftsmen who attempt it.

At the New York office at 815 Marbridge Building, Herald Square, J. George Stickley, the other member of the firm, has in charge that important branch of the Work, the placing of the finished pieces of furniture in various shops and stores where you may see and buy them. Each piece you may find, in New York or Boston, in Honolulu, South Africa, or any other of the various cities or countries that demand it, has imprinted upon it the device

The Work *of* L. & J.G. Stickley

Below are tags and marks that appear on Stickley & Limbert items.

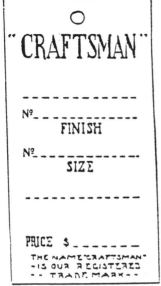

Stickley Tags

Stickley Tags

Stickley Mark (Red)

Limbert Tag

H

ROYCROFT
Furniture

Here is shown a roomy, comfortable settee, built as good as the Roycroft artisans can make it. Fashioned in oak it is five feet long, constructed in the old-time way and held together with pin and slot. Finished in either Flemish or weathered oak, as desired, the price is $30.

All Roycroft Furniture is made very solid and plain; it will last longer than we do and then be as good as new,—nor will it be out of style. If you are interested, send for our catalog.

The Roycrofters EAST AURORA NEW YORK

1903 Ad

The Magazine PEDESTAL

shown herewith has been about the best selling piece of furniture we have made. It is artistic, serviceable, and withal very beautiful. The pedestal is of oak, hand-made and is 5 feet 3 inches in height. The price is $20.00. The old carpenter has just finished half a dozen, three being in light brown and three in weathered oak. If these are all sold when your order comes, we can make you one in about ten days.

ADDRESS

THE ROYCROFTERS
EAST AURORA New York

1904 Ad

Bedroom ROCKER

LEATHER SEAT

18 inches wide, 17 inches deep. Back just high enough to rest your head comfortably.

May we send you one on Suspicion?

Oak, $12.00   Mahogany, $14.50   Ash, $11.00

THE ROYCROFTERS
Furniture Shop   East Aurora, N. Y.

1906 Ad

ALI BABA BENCH Solid oak—weathered finish. Bark side down. Polished top. Forty-two inches long

PRICE, TEN DOLLARS

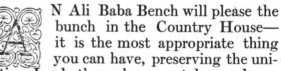

N Ali Baba Bench will please the bunch in the Country House— it is the most appropriate thing you can have, preserving the unities. Look through our catalog and you may find some other pieces you would want. Now is the accepted time! We make special pieces for that corner you are wondering how to fix up.

The Roycrofters Furniture Shop East Aurora, N. Y.

1905 Ad

I

Roycroft Morris Chair

LARGE SIZE (No. 1) 31 inches wide, 25 inches deep, 15 inches high to top of seat cushion—with velour cushions, $40—with leather cushions $50.

SMALL SIZE (No. 2)—26 inches wide, 23 inches deep, 14 inches high to top of seat cushion—with velour cushions, $35—with leather cushions, $45.

This Chair is a close replica of the original William Morris Chair. Very solid, strong, durable. Made by hand of quartered red oak lumber—thoroughly seasoned—weathered oak finish.

SEND FOR OUR CATALOG OF OTHER PIECES

THE ROYCROFTERS
FURNITURE DEPARTMENT
EAST AURORA, ERIE COUNTY, NEW YORK

1905 Ad

ARM-CHAIR

Solid Oak—very plain and massive — leather seat, twenty-one inches square, inside measurement. This same chair also in a rocker.

Price, $15.00

𝕽oycroft 𝕱urniture
Absolutely Hand-made

LIBRARY TABLE

Solid Oak—very massive—52 inches long, 33 inches wide—mortised and pinned.

Price, $25.00

1903 Ad

ROYCROFT
FURNITURE

Made to outlast the possessor, by men who have found their work, and are reasonably kind

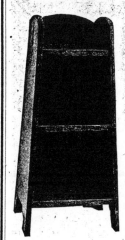

Here is a new piece recently turned out. We call it the Roycroft Magazine Rack. 36 inches high, 14 inches square at the top, 18 inches square at the base—3 shelves. Price, eight dollars to the faithful, while they last, and when they are gone we will make some more; so send along your order and we will fill it as soon as possible.

And then we also make a few other pieces for dining-room, library or den. Send for catalog and complete price list.

THE ROYCROFTERS
East Aurora, New York

1904 Ad

ROYCROFT
𝕱urniture

The accompanying illustration shows a round table of which the Roycroft carpenters have made a limited number. The table is of oak, entirely hand-made and is ornamental, as well as serviceable. In diameter the top measures 3 feet, and this piece of furniture is one that will last a lifetime and then go to the next generation as a prized heirloom. The table is finished in weathered oak, discreetly and well, and will satisfy the most particular purchaser. The price is $20.

The Roycrofters   EAST AURORA NEW YORK

1903 Ad

An article made with an eye on the purchaser is already ruined.—GEORGE WHARTON JAMES

ROYCROFT
Furniture

IS for the Roycrofters. We made forty of these chairs for ourselves, and also for you should you care for them. We call it the **Dining-Room Chair** No. 2. You may place it in your hallway, though, if your hallway is good enough. Slightly curved back, leather seat. Handmade from quartered oak, nineteen and one-half inches wide, eighteen and one-half inches deep, and forty-one and one-half inches high. Price $10.00 each—$60.00 per half dozen. Address

The Roycrofters — EAST AURORA NEW YORK

1903 Ad

IT IS A
Roycroft High-Chair

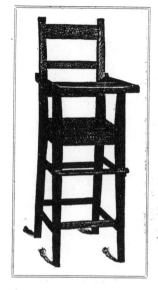

And if you have a Little Blessed to put in one, why, you could n't do better than to get one of these for a birthday present. The price is $12.50, with the baby's name carved on the back. Solid Oak and all else that's roycroftie

The Roycrofters — East Aurora, Erie County, New York

1904 Ad

Roycroft Furniture

SERVING TABLE, No. 2.
44 Inches Wide; 22 Inches Deep; 36 Inches High to Shelf

Entirely made by hand from best quality thoroughly seasoned quartered red oak lumber. Very solid and durable—finished in weathered oak.

Price, $12.00; With Drawer, $15.00

F.O.B. Cars at East Aurora

Perhaps you would be interested in our catalog showing other pieces. We will gladly send it.

THE ROYCROFTERS
EAST AURORA, NEW YORK

1904 Ad

Roycroft Bookcase
No. 085

66 inches wide   62 inches high   14 inches deep
In Oak, Seventy Dollars   In Mahogany, Eighty-five Dollars

JUST for the Very Elect Few we will still make a little **ROYCROFT FURNITURE** ¶ We have but six men, Deacon Buffum and his five sons, one with a blot on his 'scutcheon, making furniture—by hand ✄ Quality, from every standpoint: Simplicity in design, strength, beauty, durability, are the first and last endeavors. ¶ The number of orders we can take care of is limited, of course, but we think we can handle yours. ¶ Our new catalog contains illustrations of the pieces we are now making. These pieces ONLY do we make—NOTHING ELSE! But they are EXCLUSIVE—INDIVIDUAL—just for you. We will gladly mail you a catalog upon your request to do so.

THE ROYCROFTERS, EAST AURORA, NEW YORK

1908 Ad

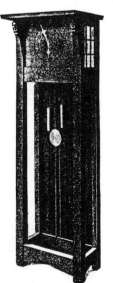

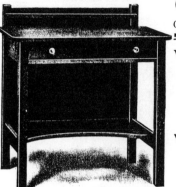

Tobey
Hand-Made
Furniture

The originality of design and the beauty of the carving that characterize Tobey Hand-Made Furniture are well illustrated in this cabinet. Furniture like this is individual. It exemplifies conceptions of art in furniture-making that result from many years of earnest study and the desire to produce distinctive things. Such pieces are not the fulfilment of a passing fancy; they embody characteristics in design and construction that enhance their value as time goes on.

Tobey Hand-Made Furniture will at all times and under all conditions satisfy the most exacting requirements. It will not only serve its present owners, but will be treasured as heirlooms in the future.

Send for our booklet,
"Tobey Hand-Made Furniture."
THE TOBEY FURNITURE CO.
Chicago
1904 Ad

THIS good-looking, substantial writing desk is made in a variety of dull-finished woods. It has a roan writing pad. With handsome waste basket it costs

$12.25

We will send you a booklet about

"United Crafts"

Furniture

It is not simply because this "Crafts Furniture" is the *dernier cri* that those who follow the newest in artistic styles select it for their homes, but also because it contains such basic principles of good taste and common sense that its permanence is assured.

Disciples of William Morris are doing wholesome work in turning out these dull-finished, restful articles for the home beautiful : tables, desks, chairs—all solid, comfortable, and delightfully logical in line and color.

There are many imitations ; write for a handsomely illustrated booklet, containing much interesting information about the craft, and some suggestive pictures of art corners, written by those who know. Sent free.

Department M 4   *Scruggs Vandervoort & Barney*   ST. LOUIS

1902 Ad

HOUSE FURNISHINGS

In a Student's Room

the most useful thing is the desk. Convenience, durability, and beauty — in the order named — are the chief requirements.

This desk would be an inspiration to work. It is made in the workshops of the

United Crafts

by men who believe in a closer union of beauty and utility.

The flat top is covered with tough roan skin, forming an ideal writing surface. It has two deep drawers and underneath is a magazine rack. Made of weathered oak, with honest joints and clean lines, it will stand years of rough college usage, and then find a welcome in your home for a generation or two.

Price $22.50   With wood top $17.00
(Freight prepaid to Eastern Points)

If you would like to read an interesting little book about UNITED CRAFTS and the CRAFT movement, it will be sent you free.

Dept. M.4   *Scruggs Vandervoort & Barney*   St. Louis

1902 Ad

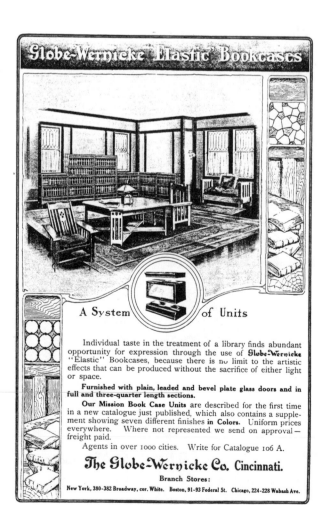

Globe-Wernicke "Elastic" Bookcases

A System of Units

Individual taste in the treatment of a library finds abundant opportunity for expression through the use of Globe-Wernicke "Elastic" Bookcases, because there is no limit to the artistic effects that can be produced without the sacrifice of either light or space.

Furnished with plain, leaded and bevel plate glass doors and in full and three-quarter length sections.

Our Mission Book Case Units are described for the first time in a new catalogue just published, which also contains a supplement showing seven different finishes **in Colors.** Uniform prices everywhere. Where not represented we send on approval — freight paid.

Agents in over 1000 cities. Write for Catalogue 106 A.

The Globe-Wernicke Co. Cincinnati.

Branch Stores:

New York, 380-382 Broadway, cor. White.   Boston, 91-93 Federal St.   Chicago, 224-228 Wabash Ave.

1906 Ad

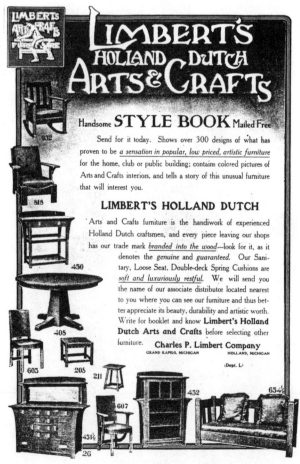

LIMBERT'S HOLLAND DUTCH ARTS & CRAFTS

Handsome STYLE BOOK Mailed Free

Send for it today. Shows over 300 designs of what has proven to be *a sensation in popular, low priced, artistic furniture* for the home, club or public building; contains colored pictures of Arts and Crafts interiors, and tells a story of this unusual furniture that will interest you.

LIMBERT'S HOLLAND DUTCH

Arts and Crafts furniture is the handiwork of experienced Holland Dutch craftsmen, and every piece leaving our shops has our trade mark *branded into the wood*—look for it, as it denotes the *genuine* and *guaranteed*. Our Sanitary, Loose Seat, Double-deck Spring Cushions are *soft and luxuriously restful.* We will send you the name of our associate distributor located nearest to you where you can see our furniture and thus better appreciate its beauty, durability and artistic worth. Write for booklet and know **Limbert's Holland Dutch Arts and Crafts** before selecting other furniture.   **Charles P. Limbert Company**

GRAND RAPIDS, MICHIGAN   HOLLAND, MICHIGAN

(Dept. L)

1909 Ad

S

Frank Lloyd Wright spindled side chair, high back chair with six vertical spindles underneath a wide crest rail extending to the bottom back stretcher, back and front feet both curve outward, leather covered slip seats. 44 3/4 "h.

Limbert hall chair #81, c.1910, a rare and spectacular example of Limbert furniture, untouched medium brown finish with branded mark. 14" w x 14 "d x 45" h.

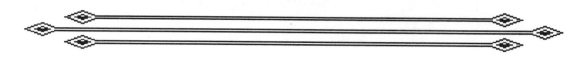

Gustav Stickley spindle chair #390, fixed back with 24 spindles under arm, beautifully proportioned, possibly the rarest of spindle chairs, leather covered cushions, branded mark with original label. 39"h x 29 "w.

Gustav Stickley box arm morris-chair #336, no mark. 40"h.

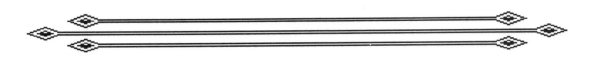

L. & J.G. Stickley arm chair #816, 6 small vertical slats back, open under arms, corbels front under arms, mortised through top arms, brown finish with burned in signature. 39"h x 22 1/2" w x 19 1/4" deep.

L. & J.G. Stickley side chair, eight spindles to the chair back, original dark finish, hand-craft decal. 17 1/2" w x 16" d x 39 1/2" h.

Morris chair, 5 slats extending to the floor, under wide arms, reclining back rest on wooden bar is style of L. & J.G. Stickley. 32"w x 27" deep x 40" h.

L. & J.G. Stickley chair #330, 8 spindles in back, not signed. 36 3/4" h x 16 1/2" w x 15" deep.

Oak Craft slatted cube chair, thru tenons, original dark finish, signed with label. 34" high x 32" wide.

Gustav Stickley V-back armchair #312, original red/brown finish, unsigned.

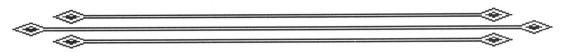

L. & J.G. Stickley morris chair #830, open arms, corbels under arms front & back, post mortised through top front & back, 4 horizontal slats back, bar for reclining chair, dark original reddish brown finish. 24 1/2" w x 43" floor to top of back x 35" deep.

Gustav Stickley morris chair #332, c.1904, early example with five slat sides, thru tenons. 23" w x 27" d x 40" h.

L. & J.G. Stickley morris chair #471, six wide slats under arm, leather cushions, branded. 41" high.

L. & J.G. Stickley morris chair #412, over-sized and comfortable paddle arm morris chair, Handcraft decal. 35" w x 26" d x 40" h.

Gustav Stickley drop arm morris chair #369, spring cushion, dark red/brown finish, leather cushions, 40" h, 24" seat width.

L. & J.G. Stickley morris chair #762, early example w/ arched sides and skirts, complemented by arched pieces under arms and corbels front and back, *rarely found chair*, 42" h x 43" l x 33 1/2" w.

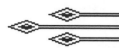

Mission Oaks arts & crafts chair, even arm cube chair with brown leather inserts on sides and back with studs, brown leather seat, 2 slats on sides, 3 in back, medium brown finish, unsigned, *well made good design.* 32" h x 20" deep x 23 1/2 "w.

Stickley Bros. cube chair, two wide slats under even arms and back, leather cushion, 30" h x 26" w x 26 " d.

Limbert bench #243 1/2, four rectangular cut-outs on each side, splay slab legs, branded mark, 24" w x 18" d x 24" h.

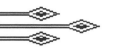

Gustav Stickley morris chair #367, c.1905, twenty-two spindles on each side of this prarie school inspired morris chair, cushion supported by original canvas sling seat, signed with Eastwood paper label. 19" w x 24" d x 36" h.

Morris chair, bow arm with rope seat, well constructed chair, pegged back, thru posts, unmarked. 27 1/2" deep x 28 1/2 wide x 43" high.

Stickley Bros. arm chair, signed twice & numbered.

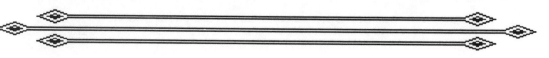

Limbert morris chair #814, deep, low substantial with massive front legs, leather cushions, early paper label. 33" w x 37" d overall.

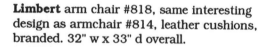

Limbert arm chair #818, same interesting design as armchair #814, leather cushions, branded. 32" w x 33" d overall.

Limbert Morris chair #520, large chair has spade cut-outs on front and sides over arched bottom, wide shaped arms are supported by corbels, leather cushions. 35" w x 40" deep.

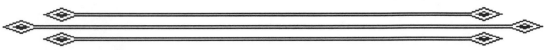

Gustav Stickley side chair #350, three vertical slats, leather seat. 39" high.

Roycroft side chair #031, c.1905, heavy high back chair, script signature at top over three slat back, *considered rare and important.* 19" w x 19" d x 47" h.

Charles Stickley arm chair, attribution, pair of corbels under arm, slats under flat arms, 4 vertical slats in back, *nice design.* 28" w x 24" deep x 37" h.

L & J.G. Stickley "Onandaga Shops" #754 side chair, no arms, 1 wide horizontal slat back and 4 smaller, pointed top horizontal pc. pinned, dark brown finish, leather cushions with cross stitching. 37 1/4" h x 19 1/4" w x 18 1/4" deep.

Gustav Stickley chair #306 1/2, heavy ladderback, dark reddish/ brown finish, leather seat.

Roycroft chair #030, high back hour-glass side chair, leather seat, orb incised on seat rail. 17" w x 16 1/2" d x 43" h.

Gustav Stickley arm chair #305A, leather cushion, red decal. 38" h x 20 1/2 deep x 26" w.

Roycroft chair, four slats to back, orb incised on seat rail. 19" 1/2 w x 18 1/2" d x 41 1/2" h.

Michigan Chair Co. mahogany hall seat, eleven vertical spindles on each side, signed paper label. 24" w x 30" h x 16 1/2 x diam.

Gustav Stickley arm chair #326, loose cushion sits on a rope seat, five slats in back, red decal. 24 1/2" w x 20 1/2" d x 37" h.

Limbert arm chair #837, large fixed back with open arms, high back with two slats, cushions. 43" h x 29" w x 32" deep.

L. & J.G. Stickley arm chair #426, bowed arm with 4 vertical slats, signed "The Work of...".

Limbert desk chair #85, upholstered seat, original red/brown finish, arched rails, arched back, burned signature. 42" h.

Gustav Stickley arm chair #310 1/2, original red/brown finish and leather seat, red decal. 36" h - 18" to seat x 20" wide x 19" deep.

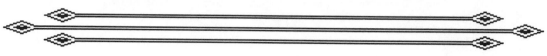

Arts & Crafts dining chairs, comes in sets of six, very good look with spindles under horizontal back with 2 square cut-outs, cane seats.

Gustav Stickley fixed back arm chair #324, five slats under flat arm, red decal. 41" high.

L. & J. G. Stickley ladder back chairs, 1 with arm, 5 only side chairs, all signed "The Work of...".

Gustav Stickley chairs #370, *desirable form* with leather drop-in seats, graceful legs taper at bottom, unmarked.

Gustav Stickley dining chairs, #340 arm chair and #338 side chairs, c.1907, Harvey Ellis influence, drop-in seats, original light finish, *beautiful and desirable design*, red decal. Armchair 24" w x 21" d x 40" h. Sidechairs 16" w x 16" d x 39" h.

Shop of the Crafters oak chairs #320 and #321, c.1906, five side chairs, one armchair, decorative marquetry panels inlaid in chair backs, paper labels. Side chairs 18" w x 18" d x 44" h. Arm chair 28" w x 23" d x 48" h.

15

4 Gustav Stickley v-back chairs, 2 arm #354 1/2, 2 side #354, all branded, paper label, leather seats.

Gustav Stickley chairs #306 1/2, set of 6, original reddish/brown finish, burned mark, leather seats, all with Eastwood labels.

Gustav Stickley rocker #323, five slats under straight arms, thru-posts in arms, spring cushion, red decal. 22" w x 25" d x 38" h.

L.& J.G. Stickley bent arm rocker #401, leather cushions, "work of..." decal.

Limbert morris rocker #518, bent arm at back, arched seat rail, thru posts front and back, an oversized and comfortable rocker, branded. 31" w x 40" d seat.

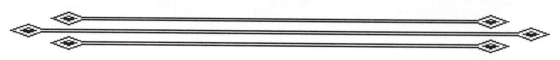

L. & J. G. Stickley rocker #827, notched top rail, leather cushion, branded " The Work of...". 27" w x 32" h x 17" d cushion.

Limbert rocker #676, c.1908, branded. 28" w x 24" d x 34" h.

Gustav Stickley V-back rocker #311, signed with red decal.

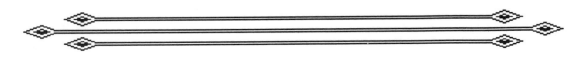

Roycroft rocker, heavy rocker with five slats to back, thick top rail, inset hard leather seat, wide armrests, original brown finish, orb incised on seat rail. 24" w x 22" d x 36" h.

Limbert #842 rocker, large, deep chair with fixed back, five vertical slats under arms, *beautiful form*, red/brown. 38" h x 32" x w x 40"deep.

Gustav Stickley rocker #319, open arm, loose cushion over rope seat frame.

Stickley Bros. rocker, rectangular caned panels under arms, 6 slats in back, brown leather cushion. 35" h x 27" w x 26 deep.

Gustav Stickley child's arm rocker #343, c.1910, 18" w x 14" d x 26" h.

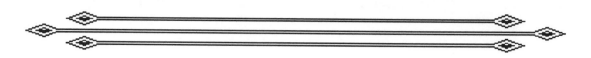

Gustav Stickley rocker #303, c.1904, sewing rocker with rope support and leather cushion, beautiful red//brown finish. 17" w x 16" d x 33" h.

L.& J.G. Stickley rocker #427, bowed arm with 4 vertical slats under arm, signed "The Work of...". 36" h x 22" w x 25" d.

Gustav Stickley V-back rocker, brown finish and rush, red decal.

Charles Stickley rocker, corbels under arm, 5 slats under flat arms, 3 horizontal slats in back. 30" w x 29" d x 34" h.

Limbert ebon-oak rocker, c.1914, oak rocker with inlays of ebony, single slat sides under corbeled bow arms, branded. 30"w x 28" d x 34" h.

Gustav Stickley H-back rocker, leather cushion. 36" h x 25" w x 18" deep.

Limbert rocker #8024, c.1905, back inlaid with organic design in copper and pewter. 26" w x 22" d x 36" h.

Gustav Stickley rocker #317, 5 vertical slats, signed red decal, leather cushion.

Gustav Stickley rocking chair #365, circa 1912, three vertical slats on back, corbels under arms, leather seat, branded mark.

L. & J. G. Stickley rocking morris chair #831, long corbels under arms, leather cushions, fine red/brown finish.

Limbert rocker #848, c.1912, deep low rocker, branded. 31" w x 27" d x 31" h.

Limbert extension table #423, c.1909, octagonal apron with full corbels and an octagonal center leg separates this piece from standard mission design, brown finish, branded. 54" diam. x 30" h with 4 leaves.

Limbert extension table #424, c.1912, very heavy construction, large overhanging top over octagonal center leg and a base of four corbelled exterior legs that connect to the interior legs with arched stretchers, three 12" leaves.
60" diam, x 29" h.

23

Charles Stickley table, massive round cross stretcher table with 4 leaves, through tenons. 54" diameter, 29" h.

Gustav Stickley table #627, c.1910, round table with light finish, arched stretchers with faceted nipple in middle, red decal. 48" diam. x 30" h.

Gustav Stickley dining table #656, round, pedestal table with five leaves, red decal and paper label. 54" diam. x 29" h.

Gustav Stickley table #634, round dining table, center leg, thru-tenons, arched cross-stretchers, two leaves, paper label and branded. 54" d x 30 "h.

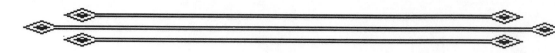

Gustav Stickley table #609, c.1907, center table with arched stretchers supporting lower round shelf, red decal. 36" diam. x 30" h.

Limbert dining table #1493, 48" top, no leaves, branded.

Stickley Brothers center table, c.1910, thick round top supported by four posts that splay to join at cross-stretcher, footed base. 44" diam. x 30" h.

Limbert cut-out table #146. 30" x 45" x 30" high.

Limbert table splayed legs, crossed stretchers with thru tenons, branded mark, 36" round, 29 1/2" h.

Gustav Stickley round table. 4-2 1/2" square legs, 48" round top, 30" high.

Limbert table #158, c. 1912, double oval table with cut-out panel stretchers, branded. 48" w x 36" d x 29" h.

L. & J. G. Stickley round table #575, small round shelf below on arched stretchers, red/brown finish. 24" diam. top x 29" h.

Limbert oval top table #146, 2 cutouts on ends, arched apron under top, reddish brown finish. Top 30" w x 45" l x 40" h.

Lifetime table, 36" top with lower shelf supported by arched cross stretchers with pegged thru tenons, no mark.

L. & J. G. Stickley two tier table #540, signed with decal " The Work of...", thru tenons, arched stretchers under bottom tier, two layered apron under splined top, red/brown finish. 24" top x 29" high.

Stickley Brothers table #2694, thru tenons, notched feet, circular lower shelf. 40" top.

L. & J. G. Stickley round side table #573, 18" top over small shelf, no mark.

Gustav Stickley round table #644, paper label. 30" diam. x 29" h.

Stickley table, beautiful form with arched stretchers and thru pegged tenons, looks like Gustav table #604, red brown finish, signed with decal. 28" h x 24" diam.

Gustav Stickley table #626, beautiful form with thru tenons and arched stretchers. 40" diam. top.

Limbert table #110, reddish/brown finish, nicely tapered legs. 29" h x 24 1/2" top.

Stickley Brothers child's table, c.1910, cross-stretchers. 24" d x 24" h

L. & J. G. Stickley #575, c.1908, tea table with 9" shelf atop arched cross-stretchers. 24" diam. x 29" h.

Limbert copper top table #109. 18" diam. x 27" h.

Stickley Brothers table #2509, unsigned, thru tenons.

Gustav Stickley table #654, arched cross-stretchers. 24" diam. x 29" h.

Limbert table#191, cross stretchers connect slightly tapered legs, branded. 24" diam. x 30" h.

Lifetime two tier table, thru tenons, paper label. 18" top x 24" high.

Gustav Stickley tea table #604, red decal mark. 26" h x 20" diam.

Gustav Stickley tea table #604, red decal mark. 26" h x 20 diam.

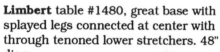

Limbert table #1480, great base with splayed legs connected at center with through tenoned lower stretchers. 48" diam.

Gustav Stickley dressing table #907, four small drawers will full strap iron pulls flank center drawer, paneled sides, mirror with butterfly joints to posts, branded. 48" w x 22" d x 55" h.

Gustav Stickley table #667, arched stretchers with finial, thru tenons, dark brown finish, red decal on leg. 30" diam. x 29" high.

Roycroft table #073 1/2, unusual form, orb signature. 30" diam. x 30" h.

Limbert table #139, octagonal top above wide legs having four square cut-outs over four long rectangular cut-outs, cross stretchers are thru tenoned and double keyed, burned mark. 48" top.

Limbert table #141, c.1910, octagonal top, wide stretchers key into four panel legs with trapezoidal cut-outs, paper label. 30" octagonal top x 30" h.

Limbert Hexagon table, cut-out spade design in splayed legs, double keyed thru tenons, flat cross stretchers, red/brown finish. 45" wide x 29" high.

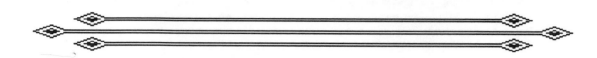

Limbert table #183, double-keyed sides, keyhole base, red/brown finish, branded and numbered. 48" w x 33" d x 29" h.

Limbert cut-out table #153, four cut-outs on sides, long corbel on side that acts as key for thru tenoned lower shelf, blind drawer, rectangular shaped top with rounded ends on each side, burned mark. 30" x 48", 30" high.

Gustav Stickley library table #616, c.1910, two-drawer library table with copper oval pulls, paper label.
54" w x 32" d x 30" h.

Gustav Stickley library table #619, c.1907, large three-drawer library table with copper hardware, red decal.
66" w x 36" d x 30" h.

L. & J. G Stickley
library table #377,
1 drawer with
hammered pulls, L.
& J. G. paper label
inside drawer, dark
brown finish.
48" w x 30" deep.

Gustav Stickley
trestle table #637,
c.1910, leather top,
double-keyed base,
paper label. 48" w x
30" d x 28 1/2" h.

Gustav Stickley
trestle table, top
supported by sides
with shoe foot
bottoms inverted at
top, thick stretcher
is thru tenoned
and keyed. 48" x
30" top.

Gustav Stickley director's table #631, large red decal, very rare. 96" w x 48" d x 30" h.

Limbert library table #1141, c.1910, two-drawer library table, long corbels, branded. 48" w x 32" d x 29" h.

Gustav Stickley spindle library table #655, rare table with 13 spindles, signed with paper label and red decal, c. 1095. 36" l x 24" w x 29" h.

Limbert library table #147, c. 1908, cut-out paneled sides with a series of corbels supporting the top, branded and numbered. 36" w x 26" d x 29" h.

Limbert library table #165, c.1912, single blind drawer, corbels support top, branded. 44" w x 30" d x 29" h.

L. & J. G. Stickley Onondaga Shops library table #1282, c.1907, two drawers with original copper hardware, thirteen spindles to each side. 42" w x 37" d x 29" h.

Limbert library table #1132, single blind drawer equipped with lift top compartment and original inkwell, legs slightly angled, arched apron, branded. 48" w x 28" d x 29" h.

Stickley Brothers library table, three slats at side with thru tenons, single drawer. 48" x 30" x 30".

Limbert table #172, long corbels, drawer on each end, lower shelf has keyed tenons, reddish brown finish, burned mark. 48" x 34" top.

Stickley Brothers library table, two drawers, tapered legs, dark finish. 52" wide x 32" deep x 29" h.

Roycroft coffee table, Mackmurdo feet joined by cross stretchers below skirted top, signed with orb, extremely rare, dark finish. 28" square top x 21" high.

Gustav Stickley library table #613, hammered pulls. Top 30" x 36", 30" high.

Gustav Stickley trestle table, signed red decal & paper label. Top 60" x 36", 29" high.

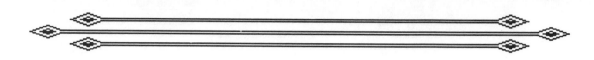

Gustav Stickley library table #651, keyed lower stretcher, signed paper label and red decal. 48" w x 29" d x 30" h.

Limbert library table #153, turtle top over a large blind drawer, long corbels serve to key the lower shelf, four square cutouts on each side, branded. 48" w x 30" d x 29" h.

Gustav Stickley library table #614, two drawers with long corbels underneath, red/brown finish, oval pulls. 48 " top.

L. & J. G. Stickley table #597, dark brown finish, hidden drawer, "Onondaga Shops" paper label. 29" h x 28 1/2" w x 40" long.

Stickley Bros. two tier table, large splined top and lower shelf, red/brown finish. Top 18" x 32" high.

L. & J. G. Stickley cut corner side table #574, c.1912, branded mark. 18" x 18" x 29" high.

Stickley Bros. tea table, legs extend through octagonal top, corbels at apron, signed with metal tag. 27" h x 20" w.

Tobey Bungalow library table, thru tenon. 1" thick top, 28" h x 29 3/4" top x 47".

L. & J. G. Stickley library table #522, single drawer, hammered copper pulls, long corbels, Hand-craft signature. 42" x 28" top

Michigan Chair Co. side table circa 1910, top above chamfered slab sides. 32" x 21" top, 29" h.

Stickley Bros. table, two drawers over one, "Quaint" tag, drop leaves. 29" l x 15" top.

Gustav Stickley sewing table #630, two drawers with wood knobs, tapered legs, red decal. 18" sq. top x 26" h. 12" leaves.

L. & J. G. Stickley drop leaf table #590, c.1912, signed, " The Work of...". Open measurements: 24" sq. top x 24" h, 8" width when leaves are dropped.

Lifetime dropleaf table #902, gate leg supports oval drops, paper label. 30" h, top 40" x 44"

Gustav Stickley drop leaf table #638, gate leg, cut corner, paper label. 30" h, 40" x 42" top.

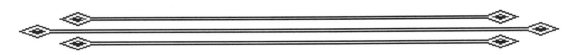

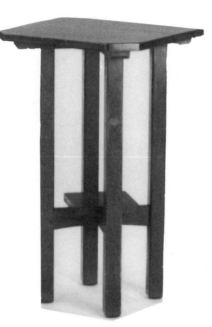

Stickley Bros. spindle sided table, tapered legs, thru tenons, three spindles each side, splined top, signed with metal tag. 34" high, 17" sq. top.

L. & J. G. Stickley half table, red/brown finish. Top 22" w x 13" deep x 30' high.

Limbert table #240, large cut-outs on each paneled side, burned mark. 20" square top x 30" h.

Stickley Bros. table, square top with flared legs and lower shelf, "Quaint" tag. 18" w x 18" d x 32" h.

L. & J. G. Stickley table, brown finish, exposed tenons. 36" diameter x 29" high.

Roycroft library table, Mackmurdo feet, dark finish, orb mark. 28" h x 22" deep x 30" wide.

L. & J.G. Stickley library table #529, single drawer with hammered copper pulls, shelf below with double keyed tenons, "Work of..." label in drawer. 29"h, 28"w x 42 " l.

Cincinnati carved table, drawer front, end panel has lilies as shown, sunflowers opposite end. 42" l x 40 1/2" h x 27 1/2" deep.

Gustav Stickley serving table #802, c.1906, two drawers over arched apron, iron v-pulls, green finish, paper label and red decal. 42" w x 18" d x 39" h.

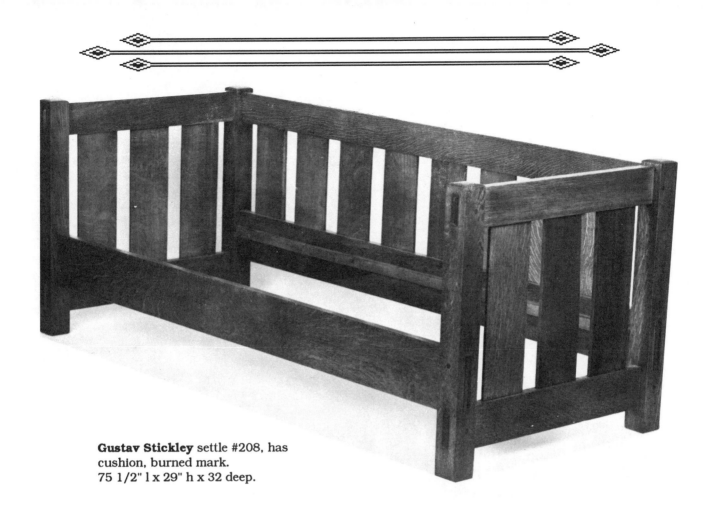

Gustav Stickley settle #208, has
cushion, burned mark.
75 1/2" l x 29" h x 32 deep.

Mission Oak Arts & Crafts even arm settle,
pointed square posts, front and back long
pieces mortised through end posts and
pinned, end pieces mortised through front
of posts and back, 2 wide slats each end, 9
vertical slats back, leather spring cushion.
67" l, 24" deep, 30" h.

Limbert settee, thru pegged tenons, 3 wide slats under arms and eight in back, unsigned.
73" w x 31" deep x 36" h.

Stickley Bros. hall settee, even arm settee with cushion and thru-tenon construction, Quaint tag. 50" w x 22 1/2" d x 33" h.

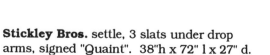

Stickley Bros. settle, 3 slats under drop arms, signed "Quaint". 38"h x 72" l x 27" d.

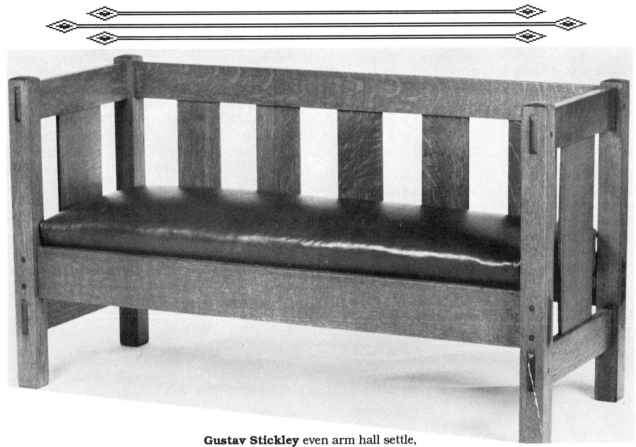

Gustav Stickley even arm hall settle,
Model 205, wide slats across back and
under arms, thru tenons top and
bottom, leather cushion. 30" h x 56" l.

Limbert settle, #559 3/4, even arm settle
with wide slats under flattened arms and
across back, has cushion, burned mark.
90" l x 34" deep x 30" h.

Limbert settee #653, spade cut outs
on sides and back slats, burned mark.
68" long, 29" deep.

Gustav Stickley slat back settee #206,
c.1904, even arms over three slanted slats,
posts taper at top, leather cushion over
rope supports, signed with large decal.
60" w, 28" d, 40" h.

Limbert settle #654, six slats to back and two canted slats to each side, unsigned. 76" w, 33" d x 36" h.

Limbert even arm settle #559 3/4, corbels under wide flat arms, 2 wide slats under arms, 5 wide slats back, burned mark. 31" h x 89" l.

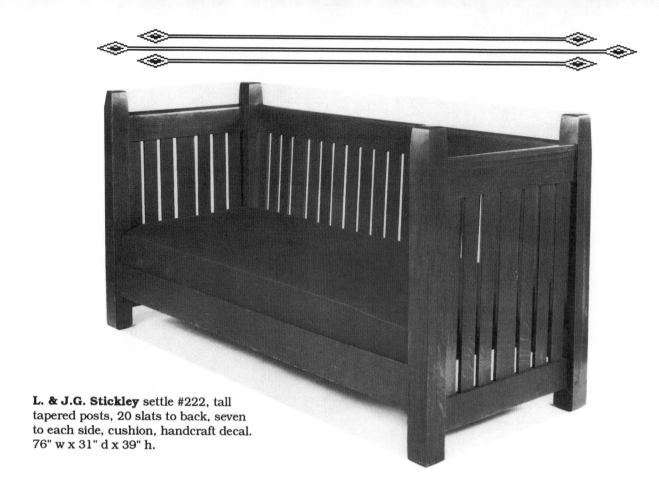

L. & J.G. Stickley settle #222, tall tapered posts, 20 slats to back, seven to each side, cushion, handcraft decal. 76" w x 31" d x 39" h.

L. & J.G. Stickley settle #223, 22 slats to back, seven slats to each side, spring cushion, handcraft decal. 84" w x 32" d x 39" h.

Gustav Stickley settle model # 225,
leather cushions and seat covers,
signed with red decal.
30" h x 31" d x 79" l.

Limbert settle # 654 1/2, six slats to back
and two canted slants to each side,
branded, has cushion. 75 1/2" w x 33" d x
36" h.

L. & J.G. Stickley even arm settle
#281, capped arms and back,
beveled edge on front seat support,
signed with decal, "The Work of L. &
J.G. Stickley". 76" l x 34" h x 31" d.

Charles Stickley drop arm settle with thru
tenons, 5 slats under arms, 14 slats in
back. 76" w x 33" d x 35" h.

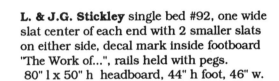

Gustav Stickley single bed #923, arched top rail over 3 wide slats, splayed legs, branded signature.

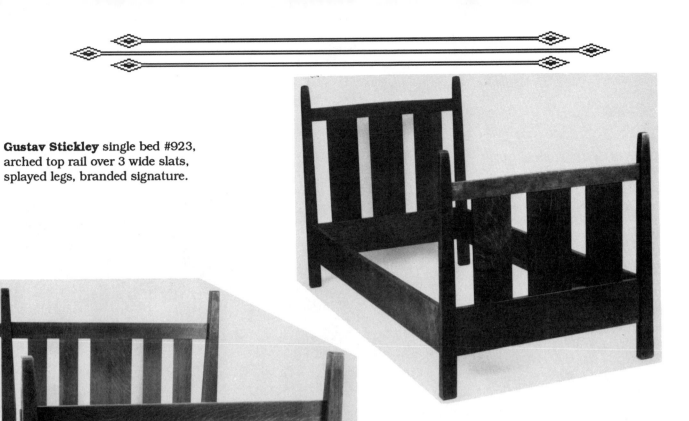

L. & J.G. Stickley single bed #92, one wide slat center of each end with 2 smaller slats on either side, decal mark inside footboard "The Work of...", rails held with pegs. 80" l x 50" h headboard, 44" h foot, 46" w.

Limbert settle #649, spade cut outs under drop arms, leather cushion, branded. 40" h x 78" l x 24" d.

Mission Oak arts & crafts day bed, slanted section at one end with 6 vertical slats at other end, 3 vertical slats on slanted side, 2 leather cushions, rectangular posts on ends. 76 1/2" l x 24" h x 27" w.

Gustav Stickley couch bed #220, c.1909, six slats at head and foot, red decal. 82" l x 36" d x 34" h.

Gustav Stickley child's bed #919, c.1905, slots in headboard, red decal. 36" w x 56" l x 44" h.

Limbert day bed #858, solid headboard, footboard has two horizontal boards, arched bottoms on all 4 sides, branded. 84" l x 33" deep.

Gustav Stickley double bed, wooden rails, burned mark, footboard 37" h, headboard 49 1/2" h x 58" w.

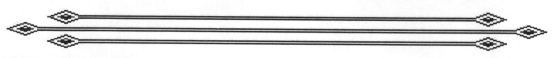

Limbert magazine rack #346, trapezoidal cut outs on side, burned mark underneath. 40"high.

Roycroft magazine pedestal #080, keyed tenons top and bottom, five shelves, incised orb and leaf design on both sides. 14" square top, 18" square base, 63" h.

Stickley Bros. spindle sided magazine stand, signed "Quaint". 39" h x 26" w x 12" d.

Stickley Bros. spindled magazine stand #4702 with four shelves, signed with paper label.

Details on page #7

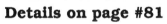

Details on page #81

Details on page #34

Details on page #58

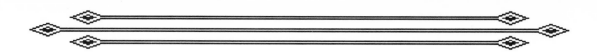

Details on page #52

Details on page #1

Details on page #53

Details on page #38

Details on page #6

Details on page #124

Details on page #65

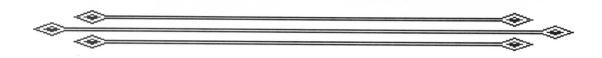

Details on page #69

Details on page #67

Details on page #28

Gustav Stickley magazine stand, c.1902, three shelves, red decal. 15" w x 14" d x 35" h.

L. & J.G. Stickley magazine stand #46, c.1910, three slats, four shelves, signed with red decal "The Work of L. & J.G. Stickley". 21" w x 12" d x 42" h.

Limbert magazine rack #302, arch in front apron, burned mark. 11" deep, 28" wide, 28" high.

L. & J.G. Stickley magazine stand #45, four shelves, arches to top, base and sides, Handcraft decal. 19" w x 12" d x 46" h.

Gustav Stickley magazine cabinet #72, arches under top and on sides, three shelves, signed with red decal and paper label. 42" h x 22" w.

Roycroft magazine rack #78. 37" h x 16" deep x 18" w.

Limbert magazine stand. 24" x 13" top, 36" h.

Stickley Bros. spindled side magazine stand #4702, three square spindles on side, signed with metal tag. 31" h x 26" w x 12" deep.

Stickley Bros. magazine stand #4600, slat sided stand. 12" x 16" x 31" h.

Mission oak cut-out bookstand, "V" top over flat shelf. 36" h x 20" w x 12" deep.

Limbert magazine stand, branded. 29" h x 16" w x 10" deep.

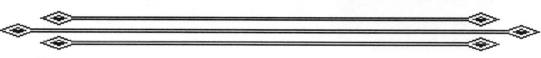

L. & J.G. Stickley magazine stand, 3 slats on each side, 4 shelves, like #46 but does not have arch on bottom, no signature. 21" w x 42" h.

Gustav Stickley magazine stand #79, small red decal. 14" w x 40" h.

Limbert magazine stand #304, four shelves above inverted toe board, burned mark. 42" h x 16" w.

Stickley Bros. magazine stand #4743, 5 shelves with single notched slat on sides, signed Quaint. 14" w x 14" d x 42" h.

Quaint magazine rack, #4602, 2 smaller slats on sides, 2 wide slats in back. 37" h x 16" w x 12 1/2" deep.

L. & J.G. Stickley magazine stand # 47, four shelves, arch on apron and sides, thru tenons top and bottom. 15" d x 18" w x 42" h.

Gustav Stickley magazine stand, carved tree of life on sides, top has corbels. 43" h, top 12 1/2" x 12 1/2".

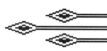

Limbert #322 bookcase, arched bottom apron and sides, thru tenons flush on sides, 2 door, 3 adjustable shelves each section, burned mark on back, round pulls. 50" h x 38" w.

Stickley Bros. bookcase #4770, double doors, 16 panes, top posts at corners, thru tenons, paneled sides, numbered. 36" w x 13" d x 52" h.

Gustav Stickley bookcase #525, double door, keyed tenons top and bottom, mitered mullions. 42" w x 12" d x 56" h.

Limbert two door bookcase #358, overhanging top above corbels and splayed legs, branded. 48" w x 57" h x 14" d.

Gustav Stickley 1 door bookcase #715, v-board back & chamfered slab sides. 36" w x 56" h.

Gustav Stickley music cabinet #70, amber glass, 2 adjustable shelves. 20" w x 16" d x 46 1/2" h.

Limbert bookcase #340, double door, 2 over 1 pane in each door, 3 adjustable shelves, gallery top, branded mark. 32" x 12" x 46" h.

Gustav Stickley 2 door bookcase
#718, 24 panes, V-pulls.
54" w x 56" h.

Gustav Stickley bookcase #542,
c.1902, double doors with mitered
mullions and iron hardware, fixed
shelves and thru tenons with paneled back. 56" h x 36" w x 12" d.

Limbert 3 door bookcase #359, splayed
legs, arched apron, no signature.
67" x 58".

Gustav Stickley bookcase, c.1903, double glass doors over double wooden cabinet, arched apron, copper hardware, 1903 decal. 42" w x 14" d x 64" h.

Limbert bookcase #350, c.1905, exterior shelves supported by corbels and paired square cut outs on each side, subtle arches repeat within the form. 30" w x 12" d x 52" h.

L. & J.G. Stickley open bookcase #642, thru tenons top and bottom, 2 handicraft decals. 55" h x 12" d x 30" w.

Gustav Stickley china cabinet #820, single door with stationary shelves, V-pulls. 60" h x 36" w.

Gustav Stickley wardrobe, c.1904, similar to #920 but larger, hooks and clothing pole inside, brown decal. 36" w x 16" d x 70" h.

L. & J.G. Stickley bookcase #643, c.1910, single door with 16 panes, double keyed construction top and bottom, handcraft decal. 39" w x 12" d x 55" h.

L. & J.G. Stickley bookcase, #645, "Work of ..." decal. 49" w x 55" h.

Gustav Stickley china cabinet #815,
double door with mirrored upper
back, arched apron, red decal.
40" w x 15" d x 64" h.

Gustav Stickley bookcase #716, c.1912, double door bookcase with thru tenon sides, stationary shelves, branded. 43" w x 13" d x 56" h.

Limbert bookcase #372, c. 1910, double door bookcase, arches at top of panes repeat in arched apron, adjustable shelves, branded. 48" w x 15" d x 60" h.

Gustav Stickley bookcase #703, double door, eight leaded panes atop each door, columns with capitals at center and sides, arched apron, red decal. 48" w x 14" d x 58" h.

Gustav Stickley book cabinet #93, early Eastwood label. 11" d x 17" w x 40" h.

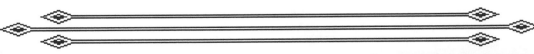

Limbert bookcase, arched door opposite two rectangular cut-outs revealing the top two of five shelves opening on the side, early paper label. 34" w x 13" d x 49" h.

Roycroft #085, triple door bookcase, keyed tenons on sides, iron hinges and round pulls with back plates, overhanging top, arched backsplash, script signature across front. 66" w x 16" d x 62" h.

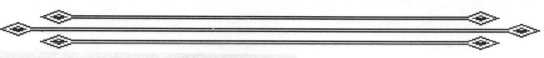

Gustav Stickley wardrobe, two doors with diamond pattern, interior is open, paper label, branded mark, circa 1912-1916.
41"w x 64"h x 24"d.

Gustav Stickley bookcase #717, double doors with 16 panes, stationary shelves, copper v-pulls, paper label.
48"w x 13" d x 56" h.

Limbert single door cut-out bookcase, open four tiered shelves on
either side extending beyond front
panels bordering door, adjustable
interior shelves, front panels with
cut-outs, paper label on back.
48" h x 12" d x 33" w.

Gustav Stickley desk #729, fall front, two drawers with added locks sit atop three long drawers, paper label and branded. 36 1/2" w x 15" d x 43" h.

Limbert desk #713, copper strap hardware, 3 drawers under slant top, burned signature. 40" w.

Gustav Stickley desk, c.1901, chestnut drop-front desk, keyed thru tenons, two drawers over one beneath drop front, shelf at bottom, complete interior, red decal. 38"w x 14" d x 48" h.

Stickley Bros. inlaid writing desk, nice gallery over slant top, single drawer with inlaid birds, early branded Quaint mark. 42" h x 36" w x 26" d.

Limbert desk table #492 1/4, two organizers form the gallery on the table top, remnant of a branded mark.
36" w x 24" d x 34" h.

L. & J.G. Stickley library desk, thru tenons, one shelf below with keyed tenons at ends, "Work of..." label on stretcher. 29" h x 28" w x 40" l.

L. & J.G. Stickley desk #660, c.1912, fall-front with two drawers over one, unsigned.
29" w x 17" d x 40" h.

Gustav Stickley desk #721, slab sides with half moon cut-outs at top, letter rack, drop leaf writing surface, thru tenon lower shelf.
29" w x 14" d x 38" h.

Limbert desk, single drawer with bookshelves on sides concealed in front by caned cut-out, thru tenon lower stretcher, branded. 42" x 26" x 29" h.

Gustav Stickley desk #708, c. 1904, desk organizer at back of flat top, two drawers over recessed lower shelf, tapered legs, signed, large red decal. 30" h x 40" w x 22" d.

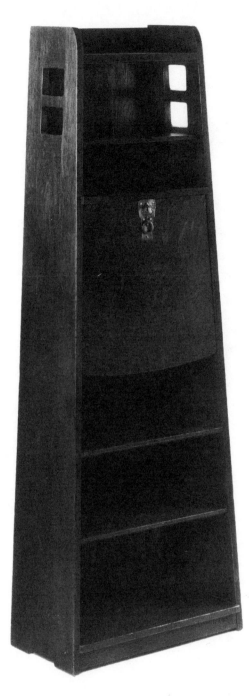

Limbert desk, c.1905, cut-out top shelves, fall front, paper label. 16" w at top, 22" w at base, 11" d at base, 60" h.

Roycroft desk, fall-front with iron strap hinges over three long drawers, script across gallery.
43" w x 17" d x 58" h.

Gustav Stickley desk #709, small red
decal, oval pulls.
29" h, top 42" x 24".

Limbert partners desk, unusual desk
with 3 drawers on each side, copper
pulls, arched kneehole, thru tenon side
stretchers, three thru tenon stretchers
running underneath.
Top 48" x 30", 29" h.

Gustav Stickley chest of drawers #906, 2
drawers over 4, full strap iron pulls, mirror
over chest with butterfly joints on posts,
panelled sides & thru tenons at bottom,
branded signature and paper label.
72" to top of mirror, 40" w, 21" d.

L. & J.G. Stickley china cabinet
#746, two doors with leaded glass
panels at top, signed "The Work
of...". 62" h, top 16" x 44".

Limbert chest of drawers #487 1/4,
5 drawers, thru tenons at top and
bottom, branded.
50" h, 36" w, 20" d.

Stickley Bros. dressing table #9013,
spindled gallery with swivel mirror,
hammered copper pulls.
55" h, 40" w, 20" deep.

Gustav Stickley chest of drawers #902, two small drawers over four large, inverted V to galley top, chamfered sides, red decal. 40" w x 22" d x 54" h.

Gustav Stickley chest of drawers #909, two drawers over three, wood knobs, red decal and paper label. 42" h x 36" w x 20" deep.

Stickley Bros. chest of drawers #9011, two drawers over three, copper hardware, slab sides, arched galley, numbered. 42" w x 20" d x 47" h.

L.& J.G. Stickley single door china closet #727. 55" h x 34" w x 15" deep.

Gustav Stickley table #645, arched cross stretchers, nippled, red decal, paper label. 36" dia. x 29" h.

Gustav Stickley dresser #627, two drawers over four, thru tenon construction, cedar interiors, early faceted iron pulls. 40" w x 21" d x 51" h.

L. & J. G. Stickley china cabinet #728, c. 1910, double door china cabinet with 18 panes, stationary shelves, arches top and bottom. 48" w x 15" d x 55" h.

Gustav Stickley dresser #905, c.1912, two small drawers over three large graduated drawers with circular pulls and vertical strap hardware, mirror with butterfly joints to posts, branded. 48" w x 24" d x 66" h to top of mirror.

Gustav Stickley dresser #911, two drawers over two, wood knobs, arched skirt and bowed legs, butterfly joint in harp, red decal and paper label. 66" h x 45 " w x 22" d.

Gustav Stickley chest of drawers #906, c.1910, two drawers over four, full strap vertical copper hardware, panelled sides, red decal. 40" w x 21" d x 48" h.

Mission Oak chest of drawers, thru tenons on bottom apron that are pegged and cut flush to post, arch in back splash. 48" h x 40" w.

Gustav Stickley dresser #626, c.1904, two drawers over three, thru tenon construction, iron oval pulls, Eastwood label. 36" w x 20" d x 43" h.

Gustav Stickley dressing table #914, two drawers with wood knobs over arched supports, butterfly joints on mirror support, slight arch in top of mirror, paper label and red decal. 36" w x 18" d x 30" h top, 54" overall height.

Stickley Bros. dresser, two drawers over two, wooden knobs, "Quaint" label. 44" w x 22" d x 66" h.

L. & J.G. Stickley pedestal #28, c.1912, long corbels, branded.
Top 13" w x 13" d x 42" h.

Stickley Bros. pedestal, square top overhangs arched apron, cross stretcher base, remnant of paper label. 14" w x 14" d x 34" h.

Stickley Bros. pedestal, four beveled feet through base. 34" h, 12" square top.

Stickley Bros. pedestal, square top overhangs arched apron, Quaint tag. 14" w x 14" d x 34" h.

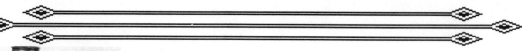

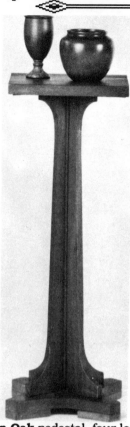

Mission Oak pedestal, four long corbels from base to top, splined top, unmarked, top 13" square.

Limbert pedestal #246, c.1905, open circular top, four curved posts splay to a large middle circle and then from four cross panels to base, paper label. 9" round top, 14" base, 43" h.

Stickley Bros. pedestal, four beveled feet through bottom of base, top and bottom are splined, burned mark. top 12" square, 27" h.

Lifetime trestle table #915, signed, numbered and paper label. 42" w x 27" d x 29" h.

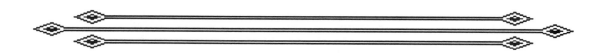

Limbert pedestal #240, c.1910, flared panel sides with cut-outs, branded. 20" w x 20" d x 30" h.

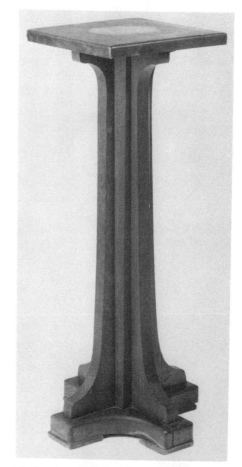

Limbert pedestal, 4 long corbals along center post supporting 13" top, branded mark. 36" high.

Limbert tabourette #191, paper label, tapered legs.

Limbert cut-out tabourette #240, square top with rounded corners with four panel sides that are cut-out, lower shelf at bottom of cut-outs, arches top and bottom, top supported by corbels on each side. Top 20" dia. , 30" h.

L. & J.G. Stickley cut-corner tabourette, #560, signed "The Work of L.& J.G...."
18" h x 16" w across top.

Gustav Stickley tabourette #602, round with arched stretchers, red decal. 16" d x 18" h.

Limbert tabourette #212, tapered legs under lower shelf, burned mark. 18" dia. x 22" high.

Gustav Stickley tabourette #603, notched stretchers, branded mark. 18" top, 20" h.

MIchigan Chair Co. tabourette, leatherette top, paper label. 27" h x 18" dia. top.

L. & J.G. Stickley cut-corner tabourette, thru posts on top, branded mark. 17" h x 15" w.

Stickley Bros. tabourette #314 1/2, thru posts flush with top, Quaint tag. 15" top, 18" high.

L. & J.G. Stickley tabourette, cut-corner tabourette with arched cross-stretchers, thru tenon legs, conjoined label. 16" w x 16" d x 18" h.

Gustav Stickley tabourette #601, marked with Craftsman label. 16" h x 14" dia.

Limbert tabourette #213, wood top over arched apron, branded. 14" w x 14" d x 18" h.

L. & J.G. Stickley tabourette #562, cut-corner top, single wide slat on every side above an arched rail. 20" w x 20" d x 22" h.

Limbert tabourette #251, long vertical
cut-outs on each side, cut corner top.
24" h, top 17" 17"

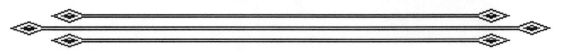

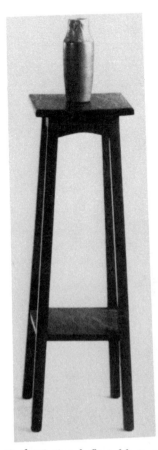

Limbert plant stand, flared legs with lower shelf, arched apron underneath 10" square top, branded mark. 33" high.

Limbert plant stand, flared legs with lower shelf & arched apron underneath 10" square top, branded mark. 27" high.

Limbert stand #214, c.1906, trapezoidal cut-outs, two shelves, early paper label. 17" w x 11" d x 34 " h.

Stickley Bros. plant stand #133, splined top over tapered legs that are thru to base, numbered. 12" w x 12" d x 34" h.

Limbert plant stand, caned panel in arched apron, inlaid ebony on legs, branded. 34" h, 14" x 14" top.

Gustav Stickley music stand #674, c.1909, legs taper at bottom, 5 square spindles at side, 7 on back, red decal and remnant of paper label. 42" h x 20" w x 14" d.

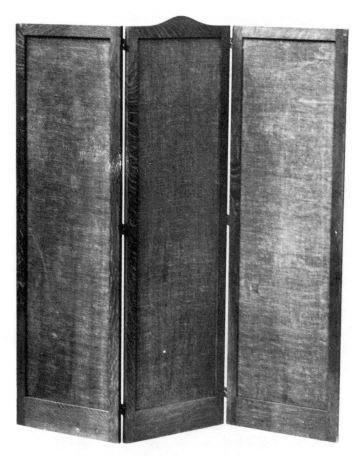

Gustav Stickley screen #83, tri fold, wooden frame, panels covered in Craftsman canvas, red decal. Side panels 66" high, middle panel 67 1/2" high, width of each 21".

Gustav Stickley plant stand #41, splayed legs, notched apron, keyed lower stretcher, early box mark. 14" x 14" x 28" high.

Gustav Stickley shirt-waist box, thru tenons at top and bottom, paper label. 16" h x 30" w x 16" deep.

Roycroft Little Journeys stand, top sits over two keyed shelves, metal orb mark, 26" w x 14" d x 26" h.

Gustav Stickley stand #641, 2 drawers with wood knobs, tapering legs, black ink stamp mark. 29" high, top 20" w x 18" d.

L. & J.G. Stickley plant stand #24, 13 1/2" w x 13 1/2" d x 28" high.

Gustav Stickley plant stand #41, c.1903, splayed legs with keyed lower stretcher, box mark. 14" w x 14" d x 28" h.

Arts & Crafts drinkstand.
20" top, 29" high.

Stickley Bros. Quaint telephone stand,
small open shelf under top, straight lines.
29" high, top 20" w x 18" deep.

Limbert trunk stand #217, woven cane
top, copper corner brackets, branded.
26" x 14" x 18" high.

Stickley Bros. plant stand #133, splined
top over tapering pedestal, legs are through
posts to base, metal "Quaint" tag.
12" x 12".

Gustav Stickley set of ten dining chairs #1297, c. 1901, u-backs with four horizontal slats to back, drop in seats, red decals.
Gustav Stickley table #627, round top with overhang, notched cross-stretchers with nippled center, red decal.

Gustav Stickley library table, hidden drawer, red decal.
Stickley Bros. tabouret, thru tenons, attribution.
Gustav Stickley umbrella stand #54, paper label.
L. & J.G. Stickley cut corner table #578, thru tenons.

Gustav Stickley library table #616, c.1912, two drawers with copper pulls, branded, 54" wide.
Gustav Stickley H-back side chair #308, branded.

Gustav Stickley arm chair #350A, brown leather cushion, red decal.
L. & J.G. Stickley footstool #391.

Gustav Stickley telephone stand #605, square top with lower shelf, branded.
Gustav Stickley arm chair #302, spring cushions, thru tenons, red decal.

L. & J.G. Stickley morris chair #498, flat arms with five slats to the floor, Handcraft decal.
L. & J.G. Stickley footstool #391, marked "The Work of...".
L. & J.G. Stickley lamp table #350, unmarked.

Limbert library table #1140, single drawer over long corbels, branded mark.
Limbert tabouret #211, 12" square top over flaring legs.

Gustav Stickley tabouret #602, arched stretchers, branded.
L. & J.G. Stickley magazine stand #47, four shelves, splay slab sides, thru tenons top and bottom, branded "The Work of...".

Gustav Stickley dining room table #656, c.1912, 54" dia. top
with four leaves, center pedestal, paper label.
Gustav Stickley ladderback chairs #349 1/2, c.1912, paper
label and branded mark.

Limbert telephone stand #272 and chair, letter
rail to back of stand, shelf under arched top,
rush seat on chair, both pieces branded.

Gustav Stickley tabourette #601, c.1910,
arched cross-stretchers, unsigned.
Gustav Stickley armchair #366,, red decal
and paper label.

L. & J.G. Stickley library table #532, two drawers with hammered copper open pulls, double keyed tenons, marked "The Work of...".
L. & J.G. Stickley arm chair #450, six slats to back and to each side, beveled seat rail, thru posts in arms, leather cushion, marked "The Work of...".

Gustav Stickley morris chair #346, open arm morris chair, red decal.
Stickley Bros. footstool, arched top, tapered legs with thru tenons.

Gustav Stickley rocker #365, leather seat and tacks, branded.
Gustav Stickley bookstand #79, four shelves, D cut-outs to top, thru tenons top and bottom, branded.

Lifetime magazine stand, 4 shelves with arches under side supports, signed paper label.
Limbert cricket stool, cut-out sides, keyed tenon, lower shelf, leather top, branded.
Limbert desk #713, 3 drawers under slant front.

Stickley Bros. morris chair, 5 slats under flat arm, thru posts front and back.
Gustav Stickley footstool #300.
Gustav Stickley bookrack #74, V shelf above flat shelf, both have keyed tenons, red decal and paper label.

Gustav Stickley child's set, 2 chairs #342 and #658, burn mark on back stretcher.

Gustav Stickley table #644, arched stretcher and center nipple, thru tenons, legs extend through top, flush on side of table, early red mark.
Gustav Stickley pair of occasional chairs #306 1/2, leather seats.

Limbert chest of drawers #484, 5 drawers with arched skirt, swivel mirror in a pegged and thru tenoned support, branded.
Stickley Bros. child's rocker, 5 vertical slats, leather seat.
Limbert single bed #511, 5 vertical slats, branded.

Mission Oak Arts & Crafts trash holder, unmarked, 4 posts with square top points, sides pinned into posts.
L. & J.G. Stickley Onandaga Shops table #597, hidden drawer, partial paper label.
Gustav Stickley v-back side chair #354 1/2, 5 slat back, burned mark.

Limbert telephone stand #261 and chair #61, slight arch to chair back, hidden braces support chair, both branded, burn to table top.

Gustav Stickley dining chairs #353, set of four chairs with
three slats to the back, drop in seats, branded.
L. & J.G. Stickley table #599, large table with keyed
stretcher, cut-out slab sides, marked "The Work of...".

Stickley Bros. morris rocker #631, flat arms
curve down at back, thru tenons, rope seat,
leather cushion, Quaint tag.
Stickley Bros. wastebasket, c.1910, cut-out
handles, thin slats.
Stickley Bros. bookcase, c.1912, double door
bookcase, posts extend above top, Quaint tag.

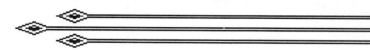

Gustav Stickley rocker #387, tall back with 3 wide slats, 3 wide slats under seat, leather cushion, burned mark.

Stickley Bros. Quaint magazine rack #4600, 3 shelves, 2 wide slats sides and back.

Gustav Stickley wastebasket #94, slats slightly wider at top.

Gustav Stickley spindle rocker #359, 9 spindles in back, red decal. 34"h x 18" w.

Gustav Stickley drugget rug, center stylized tulip design, orange and dark brown on a tan background, 7" dark brown border with zig-zag orange design. 3'11" x 2'3"

L. & J.G. Stickley rocking morris chair #831, leather cushions, burned mark "The Work of..." on back.

Gustav Stickley footstool, leather, burned mark inside top.

L. & J.G. Stickley octagonal tabourette #558, thru posts at top with arched stretchers.

Gustav Stickley dining table #656, pedestal dining table with
six leaves, paper label.
Gustav Stickley dining chairs #306 1/2, set of six ladder-
backs.

Roycroft twin bed #0106, eight slats to headboard and footboard, Macmurdo feet, box
springs have "Roycroft" woven into piping,
headboard with orb.
Roycroft dresser #0109, two small drawers
over two large ones, copper hardware, orb on
bottom drawer.

109

Gustav Stickley writing desk #708, organizer at back above 2 drawers & recessed lower shelf, iron V-pulls, signed red decal & paper label.

L. & J.G. Stickley spindled high back side chair, leather seat with copper tacks.

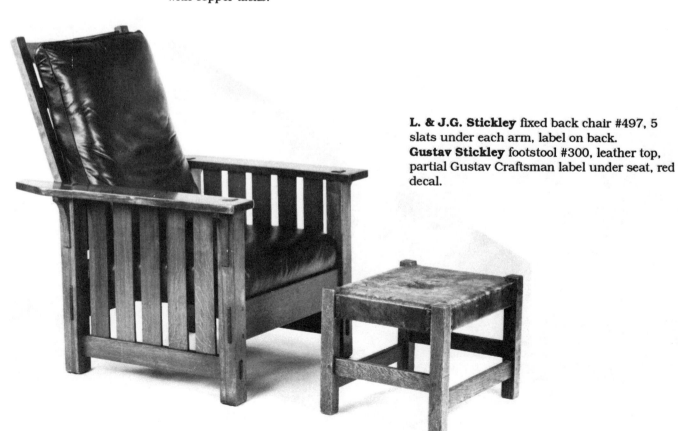

L. & J.G. Stickley fixed back chair #497, 5 slats under each arm, label on back.

Gustav Stickley footstool #300, leather top, partial Gustav Craftsman label under seat, red decal.

Limbert magazine rack #302, burned mark.
L. & J.G. Stickley footstool #391, leather, handcraft decal.
Brooks cut-out table, Limbert copy, two cut-outs each side, corbels under top.
Limbert bench arched apron under flat top, burned mark.

Stickley Bros. spindle sided footstool, leather top, unmarked.
Stickley Bros. dining table #2640, overhang over 5 straight legs, one leaf, signed with tag.

Gustav Stickley sidechairs #348, c.1904, set of
eight ladderback chairs with rush seats, early
box mark. 15 1/2" w x 15" d x 34 1/2" h.

Limbert stool #213 3/4, leather top over nice arches.
Limbert vanity #492 1/2, single drawer over arched
apron, thru tenons, branded mark.

Gustav Stickley settle #172, c.1902, a rare early example of an experimental piece of Stickley.
Gustav Stickley tabourette, arched stretcher, unmarked.

Gustav Stickley footstool #300, covered in hard lever with original tacks, red decal.
Gustav Stickley tea table #604, notched cross stretchers, paper label.
Gustav Stickley morris chair #332, five slats to the floor on each side, red decal.

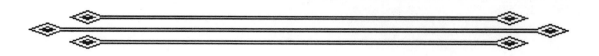

Gustav Stickley vanity #907, c.1910, five drawers, large mirror with butterfly joints on harp, red decal and paper label.

Gustav Stickley #317 rocker, red mark on back stretcher, 5 vertical slats on back.
Lifetime footstool #401, leather top, paper label on bottom.

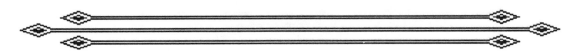

L. & J.G. Stickley table #573, round table with smaller round lower shelf atop arched cross stretchers, decal "The Work of...".
L. & J.G. Stickley morris chair #498, large flat arm morris chair, five slats to the floor, branded "The Work of...".

Limbert sideboard, two drawers over one, above two doors, paper label.
35" w x 57" h x 15" deep.

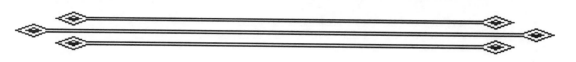

Gustav Stickley china cabinet, single door with twelve panes of glass, mirrored back, branded signature.
J.M. Young morris chair, 5 slats under arm, adjustable back, paper label.

Gustav Stickley library table #614, great design with long corbels, signed with burned mark on side of drawer & two paper labels, hammered iron pulls.
Gustav Stickley side chair #349 1/2, leather seat with round nails all around, red decal mark on back stretcher.

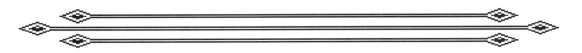

Gustav Stickley tabouret #604, without thru tenons, signed with paper label.

Craftsman style rug, dark brown & light brown design, in Arts & Crafts style.

L. & J.G. Stickley folding screen, attribution, 3 section screen with decorative print of Dutch children above 2 panels over multiple vertical slat.

Limbert rocker #508 1/2, drop in rush seat, marked, together with a Gustav Stickley mahogany rocker #337, also with a drop in rush seat and red decal.

Gustav Stickley mirror #68, 3 sections, 4 iron
hooks, paper label, large red decal.

Gustav Stickley server #818, two drawer server
with hammered copper pulls, burned mark.

Stickley Bros. hall mirror, two large hooks on either side, three smaller hooks along bottom, Quaint metal tag on back.

L. & J.G. Stickley 3 drawer server #741, signed "The Work of...".

L. & J.G. Stickley smokers cabinet, handcraft decal.

Gustav Stickley Cheval mirror #918, c.1905, bowed legs, arched, thru-tenon double stretchers, slight arch to frame top, brown decal.

Gustav Stickley umbrella stand #100, iron hoop skeleton.

Limbert chiffonier #485 1/4, two drawers over four, copper hardware, branded, with attached mirror.

Gustav Stickley cellarette #86, copper tray under flip top compartment, one drawer with hammered pull, single door with revolving tray inside.

Gustav Stickley wastebasket #94, iron hoop skeleton.

Mission Oak Arts & Crafts footstool, leather seat , 2 slats on each side, sides are 9 1/4" above seat.

Limbert cricket stool #205 1/2, cut-out sides, keyed tenon, lower shelf, leather top, branded.

Stickley Bros. chiffonier #9022, large cabinet with four small drawers atop four long drawers, copper round pulls on small drawers, open rectangular pulls on lower drawers, numbered.

L. & J.G. Stickley footstool #394, arched aprons under tacked leather top, red mark on leg.

Limbert hall mirror #24, double arm hooks at top of each side, smaller hooks along bottom, branded and numbered.

Gustav Stickley sideboard #819, 3 drawers over one, tapered legs, oval pulls, signed with red decal.

Limbert buffet #451 1/2, c.1908, floor length corbels, copper hardware with drop oval pulls relates to Limbert's cut-out furniture, six drawers, two side cabinets, French mirror, branded.

Gustav Stickley mirror #66, has four iron coat hooks, gentle arch to top, red decal.

Gustav Stickley sideboard #814 1/2, three drawers flanked by two cabinets over one long drawer, retailer's label.

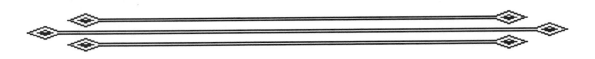

L. & J.G. Stickley footstool #391, leather top, red/brown, 18" h, 19" x 14" top.

Gustav Stickley footstool #300, c.1907, leather top, marked with red decal and paper label, matches morris chair #332. 20" w x 16" d x 15" h.

Gustav Stickley umbrella stand, 3 compartments with drip pan, tapered posts, branded mark and paper label. 34" high, 21" wide.

Frank Lloyd Wright Heritage Henredon stool, round swivel top with black leather upholstery above crossed slab base, unsigned. 17" h x 18" w.

Gustav Stickley umbrella stand #54, has drip pan and paper label. 12" square x 33" high.

Stickley Bros. wastebasket, cut-out handles and thin vertical slats, numbered on bottom. 14" w x 18" h.

Mission Oak costumer, four cut-out corbels decorate lower third applied to feet extending from base, 4 iron hooks. 6' high.

Roycroft standing ashtray #622, hammered copper, original patina. 30" high.

Roycroft hammered copper ashtray and stand with match holder on handle, signed with orb. 29" high.

Tiffany Studios bronze ashtray #1654, swirl top with two scoops for cigarettes, match holder, impressed and numbered on bottom, adjustable height.

Page 1
Top - 30,000+
Bottom - 7,000+
PAGE 2
Top - 10,000+
Bottom- 3,500+
PAGE 3
Top - 300+
Middle - 900+
Bottom - 1,000+
PAGE 4
Top - 700+
Middle - 900+
Bottom - 750+
PAGE 5
Top - 1,000+
Bottom - 4,000+
PAGE 6
Top - 1,200+
Bottom - 4,000+
PAGE 7
Top - 7,000+
Bottom - 5,000+
PAGE 8
Top - 800+
Middle - 700+
Bottom - 3,200+
PAGE 9
Top - 8,500+
Middle - 1,000+
Bottom - 250+
PAGE 10
Top - 2,500+
Middle - 1,500+
Bottom - 4,000+
PAGE 11
Top Left - 1,500+
Top Right - 350+
Bottom Left - 800+
Bottom Right - 350+

PAGE 12
Top Left - 700+
Top Right - 550+
Middle - 600+
Bottom Left - 800+
Bottom Right - 600+
PAGE 13
Top Left - 700+
Top Right - 900+
Middle - 1,500+
Bottom Left - 350+
Bottom Right - 400+
PAGE 14
Top Left - 2,500+
Top Right - 1,100+
Bottom - 1,500+
PAGE 15
Top - 1,750+
Middle - 2,500+
Bottom - 3,500+
PAGE 16
Top - 2,500+
Bottom - 3,000+
PAGE 17
Top - 1,500+
Middle - 2,500+
Bottom - 1,500+
PAGE 18
Top - 800+
Middle - 1,000+
Bottom - 750+
PAGE 19
Top Left - 900+
Top Right - 2,000+
Middle - 1,000+
Bottom Left - 500+
Bottom Right - 600+

PAGE 20
Top Left - 400+
Top Right - 2,000+
Bottom Left - 750+
Bottom Right - 800+
PAGE 21
Top Left - 1,200+
Top Right - 750+
Bottom Left - 1,200+
Bottom Right - 1,200+
PAGE 22
Left - 1,000+
Top Right - 600+
Bottom Right - 1,500+
PAGE 23
Top - 9,000+
Bottom - 5,000+
PAGE 24
Top - 2,500+
Bottom - 3,500+
PAGE 25
Top - 3,000+
Bottom - 6,000+
PAGE 26
Top - 2,000+
Middle - 900+
Bottom - 2,500+
PAGE 27
Top - 2,000+
Middle - 1,500+
Bottom - 2,000+
PAGE 28
Top - 5,000+
Bottom Left - 1,500+
Bottom Right - 2,500+
PAGE 29
Top Left - 800+
Top Right - 900+
Bottom Left - 750+
Bottom Right - 700+
PAGE 30
Top Left - 1,750+
Top Right - 1,000+
Bottom Left - 3,000+
Bottom Right - 400+

PAGE 31
1st Row:
Left - 500+
Middle - 1,100+
Right - 750+
2nd Row:
Left - 750+
Middle - 1,500+
Right - 950+
3rd Row:
Left - 600+
Middle - 700+
Right - 800+
PAGE 32
Top Left - 3,000+
Top Right - 2,500+
Bottom Left - 900+
Bottom Right - 3,500+
PAGE 33
Top - 6,000+
Bottom Left - 1,500+
Bottom Right - 2,500+
PAGE 34
Top - 3,500+
Bottom - 3,000+
PAGE 35
Top - 1,500+
Bottom - 3,000+
PAGE 36
Top - 1,000+
Middle - 2,500+
Bottom - 1,200+
PAGE 37
Top - 15,000+
Bottom - 1,200+
PAGE 38
Top - 5,000+
Bottom - 3,500+
PAGE 39
Top - 1,000+
Middle - 4,000+
Bottom - 900+
PAGE 40
Top - 650+
Middle - 900+
Bottom - 800+

PAGE 41
Top - 5,000+
Middle - 1,100+
Bottom - 3,000+
PAGE 42
Top Left - 1,750+
Top Right - 2,000+
Bottom Left - 1,000+
Bottom Right - 1,750+
PAGE 43
1st Row:
Left - 900+
Middle - 700+
Right - 800+
2nd Row:
Left - 1,000+
Right - 1,700+
3rd Row:
Left - 550+
Middle - 750+
Right - 1,200+
PAGE 44
Top - 3,000+
Bottom Left - 900+
Bottom Right - 1,700+
PAGE 45
Top Left - 1,000+
Top Middle - 700+
Top Right - 3,000+
Bottom Left - 800+
Bottom Right - 800+
PAGE 46
Top Left - 1,000+
Top Right - 1,200+
Bottom Left - 2,500+
Bottom Right - 3,500+
PAGE 47
Top - 8,500+
Bottom - 2,500+
PAGE 48
Top - 4,500+
Middle - 2,500+
Bottom - 1,200+
PAGE 49
Top - 3,500+
Bottom - 3,500+

PAGE 50
Top - 3,000+
Bottom - 20,000+
PAGE 51
Top - 3,500+
Bottom - 5,000+
PAGE 52
Top - 9,000+
Bottom - 8,500+
PAGE 53
Top - 12,000+
Bottom - 3,500+
PAGE 54
Top - 9,500+
Bottom - 3,500+
PAGE 55
Top - 2,000+
Middle - 3,500+
Bottom - 1,200+
PAGE 56
Top - 1,250+
Bottom - 8,000+
PAGE 57
Top - 3,500+
Middle - 900+
Bottom - 3,000+
PAGE 58
Top Left - 3,500+
Top Right - 4,500+
Bottom Left - 800+
Bottom Right - 900+
PAGE 59
Top Left - 3,000+
Top Right - 1,200+
Bottom Left - 600+
Bottom Right - 2,000+
PAGE 60
Top Left - 2,000+
Top Right - 3,000+
Bottom Left - 850+
Bottom Right - 1,100+
PAGE 61
Top - 750+
Middle - 300+
Bottom - 500+

PAGE 62
Top Left - 700+
Top Right - 1,750+
Bottom Left - 800+
Bottom Right - 600+
PAGE 63
Top - 700+
Bottom Left - 1,200+
Bottom Right - 800+
PAGE 64
Top Left - 2,500+
Top Right - 1,200+
Bottom Left - 4,000+
Bottom Right - 2,500+
PAGE 65
Top - 3,000+
Middle - 6,000+
Bottom - 2,500+
PAGE 66
Top - 4,500+
Middle - 3,000+
Bottom - 2,000+
PAGE 67
Top Left - 19,000+
Top Right - 4,000+
Bottom - 1,500+
PAGE 68
Top - 3,000+
Bottom - 3,000+
PAGE 69
Top - 3,500+
Bottom - 4,500+
PAGE 70
5,000+
PAGE 71
Top - 3,500+
Bottom - 3,000+
PAGE 72
Top - 9,000+
Bottom - 4,000+
PAGE 73
Top - 7,000+
Bottom - 8,000+
PAGE 74
Top - 9,000+
Bottom - 4,500+
PAGE 75
7,500+

PAGE 76
Top Left - 3,000+
Top Right - 3,500+
Bottom Left - 3,500+
Bottom Right - 1,500+
PAGE 77
Top Left - 1,200+
Top Right - 1,200+
Bottom Left - 700+
Bottom Right - 1,500+
PAGE 78
Top - 600+
Bottom - 1,100+
PAGE 79
Top - 3,000+
Bottom - 6,000+
PAGE 80
Top - 1,500+
Bottom - 3,500+
PAGE 81
Top Left - 8,000+
Top Right - 5,000+
Bottom Left - 2,000+
Bottom Right - 1,100+
PAGE 82
Top - 4,500+
Bottom Left - 3,500+
Bottom Right - 2,500+
PAGE 83
Top Left - 4,000+
Top Right - 2,000+
Bottom Left - 4,000+
Bottom Right - 4,000+
PAGE 84
Top - 6,000+
Bottom - 4,500+
PAGE 85
Top - 7,000+
Bottom - 2,000+
PAGE 86
Top - 5,000+
Middle - 3,500+
Bottom - 2,000+
PAGE 87
Top Left - 3,000+
Top Right - 1,000+
Bottom Left - 500+
Bottom Right - 800+

PAGE 88
Top Left - 500+
Top Right - 2,000+
Bottom Left - 800+
Bottom Right - 800+
PAGE 89
Left - 5,000+
Right - 3,000+
PAGE 90
Top Left - 600+
Top Right - 3,000+
Bottom Left - 800+
Bottom Right - 600+
PAGE 91
Top Left - 800+
Top Right - 700+
Middle - 350+
Bottom Left - 800+
Bottom Right - 600+
PAGE 92
Top Left - 700+
Top Right - 800+
Bottom Left - 700+
Bottom Right - 900+
PAGE 93
3,000+
PAGE 94
Top Left - 600+
Top Right - 500+
Bottom Left - 1,200+
Bottom Right - 900+
PAGE 95
Left - 7,000+
Right - 2,000+
PAGE 96
Top Left - 3,500+
Top Right - 600+
Bottom - 5,000+
PAGE 97
Top Left - 1,200+
Top Right - 600+
Bottom Left - 600+
Bottom Right - 1,500+
PAGE 98
Top Left - 350+
Top Right - 500+
Bottom Left - 750+
Bottom Right - 1,000+

PAGE 99
Top:
A. 3,500+
B. 3,000+
Bottom:
A. 750+
B. 350+
C. 600+
D. 750+
PAGE 100
Top:
A. 4,500+
B. 500+
Bottom Left:
A. 400+
B. 350+
Bottom Right:
A. 800+
B. 1,500+
PAGE 101
Top:
A. 3,500+
B. 600+
C. 2,500+
Bottom Left:
A. 900+
B. 400+
Bottom Right:
A. 700+
B. 1,500+
PAGE 102
Top:
A. 5,000+
B. 3,000+
Bottom Left:
1,000+
Bottom Right:
A. 400+
B. 700+
PAGE 103
Top:
A. 2,000+
B. 450+
Bottom Left:
A. 1,500+
B. 400+
Bottom Right:
A. 800+
B. 1,500+

PAGE 104
Top:
A. 1,000+
B. 600+
C. 1,750+
Bottom Left:
A. 3,000+
B. 800+
C. 1,750+
Bottom Right:
   650+
PAGE 105
Top:
A. 3,000+
B. 700+
Bottom:
A. 2,000+
B. 350+
C. 1,250+
PAGE 106
Top:
A. 300+
B. 1,100+
C. 500+
Bottom:
   800+
PAGE 107
Top:
A. 1,500+
B. 3,500+
Bottom:
A. 2,000+
B. 400+
C. 1,200+
PAGE 108
Top:
A. 900+
B. 750+
C. 1,750+
D. 800+
E. 500+
Bottom:
A. 1,750+
B. 800+
C. 950+

PAGE 109
Top:
A. 4,500+
B. 2,000+
Bottom:
A. 2,000+
B. 2,000+
PAGE 110
Top:
A. 2,000+
B. 1,500+
Bottom:
A. 2,250+
B. 950+
PAGE 111
Top:
A. 750+
B. 600+
C. 600+
D. 650+
Bottom:
A. 750+
B. 1,200+
PAGE 112
Left - 3,000+
Right:
A. 400+
B. 1,200+
PAGE 113
Top:
A. 3,000+
B. 600+
Bottom:
A. 1,000+
B. 900+
C. 5,000+
PAGE 114
Top - 4,500+
Bottom:
A. 450+
B. 300+
PAGE 115
Top:
A. 700+
B. 4,000+
Bottom - 2,000+

PAGE 116
Top:
A. 4,500+
B. 1,500+
Bottom:
A. 1,100+
B. 400+
PAGE 117
A. 1,000+
B. 250+
C. 1,000+
D. 750+
PAGE 118
Top- 2,750+
Bottom - 4,000+
PAGE 119
Top - 600+
Bottom - 2,500+
PAGE 120
Left - 6,000+
Top Right - 2,000+
Bottom Right - 1,500+
PAGE 121
Top Left - 1,750+
Top Right - 3,000+
Bottom Left - 1,500+
Bottom Right - 500+
PAGE 122
Top Left - 2,500+
Top Right - 600+
Middle Right - 800+
Bottom - 800+
PAGE 123
Top - 3,500+
Bottom - 5,500+
PAGE 124
Top - 2,500+
Bottom - 4,000+
PAGE 125
Top Left - 400+
Top Right - 1,100+
Middle Left - 950+
Middle Right - 600+
Bottom Left - 700+
Bottom Right - 600+

PAGE 126
Top - 550+
Bottom Left - 1,250+
Bottom Middle - 1,500+
Bottom Right - 1,000+

Don Treadway Gallery
2128 Madison Road
Cincinnati, OH 45208

✔ **Expertise** - Our expertise in the field of the 20th Century objects is second to none. The prices we obtain can attest to that.

> We buy outright or auction on your behalf. Call us for our estimates.

✔ We want to purchase outright or take objects on consignment for our future auctions. One piece or a collection are of interest. We can arrange delivery or personally pick up objects throughout the country.

✔ We have an established international clientele base that we feel is the best in the business. That clientele has enabled us to establish many world record prices. Give us a call if you have anything to sell or consign. Thank you.

✔ **Commission** - Sellers are charged 15 %. These terms are flexible for special consignments. If someone quotes you a lower commission rate you will probably receive a lower price. You usually get what you pay for.

✔ **Payments** - Payment is made in 30 days or less. Most consignors are paid within two weeks of the sale.

✔ **Catalog** - Our catalogs are exceptional. Please compare our 20th Century catalog with our competition to judge for yourself. This quality is a key to our success.

✔ **Advertising** - We advertise worldwide and maintain the largest and most active mailing list in the industry. We advertise in ways our competition hasn't considered.

✔ **Insurance and Illustrations** - Consignors will be pleased to note that there is no charge for insurance or illustrations. Our catalogs usually contain numerous color photos.

✔ **Estimates** - We invite you to bring or send photographs of your property for our estimates. Evaluations of the property can be conducted in your home by contacting our gallery at (513) 321-6742. In Chicago, contact John Toomey at (708) 383-5234